William P

Watchwo

William Fuller

Flood Editions

Watchword

hicago

Design and composition by Quemadura Cover illustration: Sam Prekop, *Open Air*, 2005, courtesy of the artist Printed on acid-free, recycled paper in the United States of America First edition This publication was made possible in part through a grant from the Illinois Arts Council, a state agency. Some poems in this book have appeared in *Chicago Review*, *Crowd*, *Edinburgh Review*, *The Gig*, *LVNG*, and *Mark(s)*. "Near Minglewood" was published as a chapbook by Bronze Skull Press.

William Fuller received his PhD in English from the University of Virginia in 1983. He is the author of a number of books and chapbooks, including *The Sugar Borders*, *Aether*, *Sadly*, and *Avoid Activity*. He is chief fiduciary officer of the Northern Trust Company in Chicago.

Contents

2

3

PIM. *Thou seemest not to have understood what thou hast heard.*

tchworc

Watchword

What a curious world means something else when we actually sit down to study it. Have you a coppy of that booke?

a seed of air

Ode (at Work)

Head on shoulder, *Pamphilus*, fascinated by muttering? Why not remove any doubt, however academic, as to the validity of the transfer? If possible, avoid committing funds. The delay between January 31st and February 5th is offered in sympathy to all earthbound travelers, to frame them between true and false. How many things we do that are uncertain, and how many more to come— puzzling, variable, frail, injudicious, unintelligible, wrong. This is the regression to nightmare. Hotter and hotter, the door begins to melt, revealing a small causeway over the investments in continuity and tenure. What will eventually prompt a sale? Kinetic indulgence. Having attended law school, they could not be imposed upon; so we decided to vote their shares. *I won't do anything except in the most shameful way*. I remember that very well, after hours on the phone. Tell me whether seeing consists in opening and turning the eyes? Welcome to town, reviling words. Your laws shall not reach to oppress us any longer. One million five hundred thousand reasons to die; beds, leaves, blankets, looking back from afar. Consult my small plastic head—she's about to explode. *Pamphilus*, you work in *this big office*? While I pronounced these words I could detect a faint smile at the window behind me; then the floor started to shake. I have never called this a memory. But

I could talk of nothing else. Now after two years of patient silence, I am still haunted by it. The writer hereof does require that your inferences be removed from his sight. The junkyard in the sun, the milky haze, the standing water, for their work is threefold. And it affects me more than anyone. And I will speak for you without compensation. And together we will pathetically enumerate. And homage to the great red dragon. And thanks to our partners in Attrition Management. And take this bloodstained broadsheet. And do I smell bacon? For the sun makes everything crystal-clear. For covetousness is all.

Parson Platt

theft, cheat, wrong or iniquity
dance with joy displacing
emphasis viewed fully in these
shapes that find their broadest
dreams roaming throughout
leafy mazes or pressing on
from the arbor in spasms
toward three starved cows—
at the beginning it was not so
handmade goods for all
during times of roasted meats
clustered in the woods like a navel
in trance and out of trance
a former friend of mine
was afraid to approach
without distinctions
imprinted on my face
we sat together limpid and cool

Near Minglewood

so much disturbing in this blot
your eyes reaching over
to cheat power
slowly the transferor jumps
scraps of paper taste soft
in this bedding of earth
the more vacant he was
the more distraught
drawn into the Away
if it could be worked out
pragmatism literally
peels off his shoes
to eat rare flowers
out of a duty owed open fields
trees, rivers, sunlight, clouds
and hope is foaming pain

I have seen umber feelings on wing
of the first rise, easy and clear
and explained in deeper woods
what twinges gave trembling

so-called influence of sacred design
and know what it felt like
to be audible influences on those
who remember a name unaware
looking at him in his own shape
years ago, the black rat snake—
saw today a cavity in the sun
and shells of hours ripe and falling
and "death as an animal consequence"
or mudless pool

when I last studied them
they were characteristic of their kind
mouth open to fullest extent
letting in green water
like an eel swimming
through cool air above the trees
the moon grew to three times
the size of a pressed leaf
split into ponds, wide flowing,
without acquisitions, not
hesitant, to the left of switches
painting the cars or piles of tires
where would I if I hesitate
the smoke rises it is morning
full of rust along the dry rim
snatches of words, he sits

too close upon returning
the passing clouds
mirrored on his coat
the darkest road in the sky
comes leafing down

biting the reed
of bruised passages
he removes his hand from the bowl
then up spoke his own sheet
of pitted concrete
the two of them have
expressed themselves
through gently soaked wires
and fine sand
with no inclination to proceed
they stayed there
not known in prospect
the streetlamp
sat cross-legged in the sky

I was born in the desert
and remain silent
I have a place in this garden
permeable, with blue roots
forming harps of flowers
and seated myself apart

where cold has eaten
through rocks
called jewels
of tear-stained, paler color
black candle
immersed, or lined with grass
osier echo fathom
tell me again on that occasion
who stood to one side
the crickets in the plains
and fields were shouting
the water crashing
the shades pulled down low
and all day long I saw
from inside the green flame
where willows were thickest
and standing pools shivered
midway down the slope
of what you interrupted
when the train comes along
making a scraping noise
covered up like neckbones
so natural and flowing I'll
meet you at the station
near the bottom of the hill
when the pavement dries
to the left of the sun

I omit your words
blending together just now
ecstasy of my writings
in gardens copied out
at seedtime
along the edge of shadows
something like fish
their minds earthed-up
to glossy shapes
in waves or curves
of another atmosphere
most lovely rain of all
seated on concrete tufts
long rows of trees
walking through the park
and into the fields
since the frost began
objectively, eating
nothing but the skin
of the box, the paper skin
robed in wood
the terms of this delegation
are excessively beautiful
so he sent off
the floating one
to seek alms
coming behind the train

with panpipe—
do you ever see him now
in August or July
calmly engaged in song
at the squirrels' feeding ground

I went down to Huntsville
with my arms outstretched
for crossing the sea
and I have never met
never feared anyone
all else being
involuntary
ultra serene
knee-deep
at the beginning of June
preferring to dress simply
or rake up
neat oblong renderings
of many seasons
just standing there
blades of root
dug from the meridian
where plants emerge
with so much of self intact
and whether in future state
not to deny them

and their eyes
drop to the ground
one or two
blossom dark green
felt by them for others
not seen here but
watching
in the middle sky

From Pope's Letters

My poor Father dyed last night
this morning there's a mist
and someone is racing up the street
the lion in the ambulance
the lion who wrecked the hospital
esteem I never had for him
I found it not

                    his wooden leg

he stands on his head
and there he rests
resembling a seal or a ghost
in a graveyard fed by water and earth
it shines forth substratum
"glorious imaginary perpetuities"

Accidie

When to be obsessed not whether is what leads the brain away, buzzing with distortion, encased in a present exempt from increase or decrease and whose image awaits you, its purpose having been realized. Now I'm cold and have to linger. *If you don't believe I'm sinking* look at the ice—the lights in the darkness extend themselves after the trajectories of your original expression—if anything the cold is worse and steals into my shoes (which are made from small books). My eyes won't close and my breath drifts into leaping snow. You're lucky not to have required I know not what loveless waltz on the river not yet frozen and if I live on, on glass, I will hear those sounds forever ... *o mule in the alley / its / burnt unutterable name*—who calls down the jake-leg snake to immobilize it. On the bridge the air stands at needle. Dead skin wraps the whole body of darkness. Then all runs clear—the concrete and the clay are streaming through me, supplemental life forms. Coevals chatter deep. Arise teachers and appropriate the jasmine groves. In glazed winter ditches, river-crusts glitter. Look out Willie Steele, all kinds of creatures inhabit you.

Rhosymedre

Some place to find where an experience can be reproduced before
the shade escapes our longing for it, in the rumba's glow—chil-
dren calling out names they venture forth with sandwiches, and
if I had turned away they might not have come back, so I went
looking for other amusements to conjure up paths to follow them
of places
they could love
be one
I took a picture of it as it disappeared into the dark an impression
of distance and regret—late morning, late afternoon, nothing to
distinguish them—office at corner bright lights all day it was pro-
posed they offer me someone's conceptual universe in full ex-
change for random hours. When the children returned there were
stones inside the roots roasting over fires

Dives & Lazarus

FOR BONNIE BARBER

There are two articles called Article Ninth
in them would still
be
holding and effective all the
provisions not negated by them
and these giving rise
to vexations
I could not have guessed at
but not even a hint of this falls to earth
deaf as ever
I made my way through the transformation unit
past thinning crowds raised in ditches
and I felt his presence
carefully cut to fit the frame
and out of this flies a kind of bat
on a perfectly level flight path
toward all kinds of people, apparently silent,
what is their common characteristic
with some exceptions many of them
have considerable accumulations
or bear witness to pure mysterious gold
in an effort to sustain themselves

For Your Astral Pleasure

The future

can be called a conflict your role is

scrambling

if you can spare

an apple

one for each of the secondary senses

more for being good than could not fall

to worse and now expect

to enter a defensive

phase—the lambent mind

surrenders to an existence essentially personal

made up of small electric parts

displaced by the clear bodies of primal opposites

overlooking a shallow pond

and shade trees

derived from the words hate and greed—

from there it drifts on unconcerned whether the line that's

held the access has been disturbed by a question

or by an assumption on which a question

has been based—who believes in the

unseen may produce the same effect

In Memory/Mousgrove

it seems clear you are still
hoping to identify the source
of the error then renounce
any claim to it physically
in nature some hints of this could
have been discovered beforehand
lean over the rail here's my
camera out of range the haze
is green yellow paint on trees
soaking the gravel straining to
suppress laughter as you
approach the sanctuary
all due proportion is engrossed
by those stainless blossoming
out of their own heads
eat thereof and drink refreshed
enter his perforated gates
with dignity and excellence of
knowledge and without drowsiness

The Chapter of the Sheep

The application of a particular religious view together with bene-
fits conferred by terrene wisdom appear to be responsible for the
repealing of certain ordinary kinds of human behavior; this un-
avoidable inconvenience follows: force (*which we call equity*) runs
back among adjoining shadows to issue a certificate, according to
the pattern we observe when ice retires and the truth is resheathed
in a variety of interests. Some prefer that minds and things start
over again, abstracted from the need for self-defense, or that sa-
cred and venerable threats maintain no direct connection to the
added element simply understood as *drinking*. Neither can we rest
secure after having renounced everything except what intrudes on
first principles, reshaping them at the base of the baobab tree. Our
constant exposure to sun can hardly be upheld any longer. "I know
that," Margaret says, thinking of an earlier, less arid time; so a
slight doubt is elevated just beyond the desert leaf, as if it were un-
caused. No compulsion can be valid against daylight ominously
shuffling darkness into acute self-consciousness—some forty
persons have petitioned so far and I myself have made my voice
heard in ideas close to theirs, uncongealed at the center; then they
took out a cord and tied my hands—

love transfixed
by flying generalities
when the lofty and discursive
narrow to what is nearby
indigo arachnid howling
to crush them into knife points

Work of the Beast

them

       tremble where they were

similar to a paste pits cans jars

to them incline with hesitation

committed against the head

supremely excellent sparkles again

rude chords spread rich rays

the brighter pooles crave only strength

to wake their venom, pardons nearby

forfeit nothing, half-gagged

retroactively condemned

to be born turning green

celebrated sensible razor

cuts for slow extended motion

must now go search for it

Goshen

spiny paths once a hand
or cluster of them

how do they apply the
curve of the turnpike

the feeling of lace the
setting out of a caravan

not for us rapid motion
that come from worms

floating in lamplight
cold and clear

some few refuse to
jump all these geese

swimming in the
opposite direction

Enquiry

aside pandemonium fronts
early and savage utility

self-denial opposes
freedom from pain

mourning dove flat common
redpoll less conceivable

without local presence the stairs
are no longer beneath me

moving through my body
my shadow in this world

and more you would have seen
a tree of branching leather

five or six feet beyond
all prior reasoning

Other Minds

what is the use of the word
true we are housed

in an amusing shape
if she's ready, then

steal grass for her
but in ordinary life

this never happens—
great stone tropes

experiment with light
the pure efflux of

flowering earth
earth, earth—

it must compete
to be true

Traherne

Rivers Springs Trees Meadows
in my mind's eye Clouds Air

Light Rain seemed tending
and gliding toward poles of

self-preservation, you were
nothing before you came into

being, you become nothing
when you have ceased to be

a few evenings later only
absurd things survive

the arbitrary bells
move steadily away

the sea lays out
a deep gold fringe

2

The Same

The people desire their ways be looked into
but won't come up with any names
at the end of night they will have
assisted one another in the behalf of
a vehicle by which they can progress
over four hundred acres before
refusing to recognize the consequences
that border on that field,
which has been inaccessible to me
during the time of great conjunctions
in the external forms of the sky—
to wash clean this house
I swore I wouldn't act
directly on nature
using double brackets
what kind of experience might we have?
something like the following
falls for many hours—
how did it used to be said
misery Pharaoh the covetous horn
did you learn this as you convalesced

an inward-looking species, with limbs
of some huge giant, and two white eyes
in rhythmical succession
of smoke and fire
as soon as they are stripped of their bark
they travel off to death
but what you declare
when left alone
seems still
to persist

a colorless liquid with a subtle taste

I grow curious at its inclusion
I remember thinking one thing
I received it not from men
I ask who is revealed
since those persons were born too late
and naturally of the earth
or elsewhere than in the mind

The Different

And you who are
when you were going to be
not a line of this work
but a sacrifice

unplanned and without comfort of
significance, where all might set forth
their views facing the clock, should
this come to be concealed;
dog nearby sucked up into the great
silence of the ancient decorative order
spun out from moisture and silver white
all agents present, if they exist, various
reciters not having mentioned them;

snow
          and light steam
saw someone through firelight
by day seeking out stems

and none to one side
spreading tables of earth

in early morning
hills and temples
with no original parts

how timid
would evening come
and what remains able to talk
now swells
        to the west
windows crowded with
special properties
and sat together
against them, indicating a small space
inside,
        to unshade
eyes turned
austere,
resistant to all
luminous varieties

Lie down, Article Eighth,
propagated on regionally
distinct materials
whose rapid nervous acts

do not enter this phase
I'd follow

the black–and–white trees
whence they originate
deep zoned, pushing lightly
into the brain
Padma responds
the mind is open
sprang forth as a flower
and fields of fragrant stars

a little redness along
the edge of the path
gently animates dried fruit
long after sunset lingers
a class of tones
sheds in a mist
and frozen streams
draw nearer the roof of the mouth

most voices are false
therefore lie still
                    to
look on yonders wall
discountenancing itself
in ascending orders of darkness

neither arts of prophecy

nor smoked fish

had asked you

                outstretched

one of three things, evasively

Near Nod

When I was the age of three in the sultry heat the weeds were blossoming and I looked off to the east. Cut from stone, my hand strained for the wall. Long ridges of corrugated steel shot past, moving south to north. And there stood a man upon whom the sun had descended. Later my hand grew fluent of speech, and approached me, quiet and unpretending, laid out on the earth to dry.

Plat

A more broadly based plan emerged
from a substantial increase in pressure
to override traditional imperatives
under violent attack—like water
in a leaking ditch what does
it profit to read waste for want
in tune with how trade moves
through the corn and weather
to restore this glorious fabric?

Another aspect grew of
its own momentum
independently of climate
when blossoms and flowers
were at their pride and fullness
before ceding control
to meadows of relinquishment
(as I have known them in March or April
when they would weaken me)—
scavengers doubled the rate
at which flaws were detected

and those deprived of learning
learned to struggle on by themselves
quietly scheming against
coherence of goals and means
with a heart of flesh round
like a ball or egg shaped
till all the fat is dried
inside bodies of fishes
and they become prized
if desiccated lumps

Primordial consensus
then rose in its own firmament
drawing out its prey
from shallow chambers
meant to shelter those
set aside for such work,
noted above—in a thick
wood dappled vagueness
could not modify them

Red Sea

by means of an exact copy have faith to understand this negation of prejudice concerning that former time when the field was inconceivable, solitary, sightless, in Egypt or Abyssinia, roaming back and forth we studied the pain and her tongue's bleeding was how it looked to us, squinting through sandstone gates at daybreak

high, wide, and beautiful, like a sea that sings in the clouds, whose function is to be everywhere dissolving in ripples

Homburg

Already confirmed in his preeminence by the public's judgment, which would finally determine who should be modified, he inserted his violins into the head of a seraph, close to the outer edge of MI3, where they protruded somewhat, being placed slightly less than upright; later he wrote a mortgage in deference to the difference, but nothing further forthcoming despite possession of his full vigor, he placed it in default; his mind, being noncreated from morning till night, was raked out of water; and his determination to reverie would pass to its final rest in a lustrous varnish of soft twilight; feeling his great loss he made no reply except through the art of label making where he excelled all others in convulsions purified with ice

Riding North

was it track twelve now swings wide
our first stop is an apology
whether to distill that quintessence
indestructible, perfect, complete
somehow pouring from the upper deck
I sleep in the sea and clouds
capable of only two activities
which began at the age of seven
the soul is making a drink from external things
which came to know it because not akin to it
the silhouette of a bird in flight
or does it permit such speculation—
the great sea bear jabs with its tongue
extracting a strange glow
based purely on what the document says

quickly the ship—
stands against reverence for authority
because not intelligible
a repetition of the forms of doubt
a hunting scene with warplanes on the roof

a man outlined in white lights, walking or dead

who comes in to see these books

then pauses on the grate

to inspect his own hand

I feel the back of my neck alive

with an entire conjectural system

which explains my lingering here

under the blocked beams of the dissipating sun

looking only one way, which

is the direction we're taking

said

    age, agues

the rain is everywhere

steadily pressing on

luxury portion of lot

displaying remorse for not having gone there

or for not having left from there

glued to the center

the unconditional regularly opposes the conditional

here they sleep

the rites of time

you may turn your face continually

your eyes may shine in the distance

the sky may reach into a vast interior—

I had a mind to a sea voyage

not a transformation

what would the grammar support
if I could tame it
I had a mind to cold pie
deeply hung with woods
and arrows, Eros, in this (burnished) bag
with a black-capped chickadee
heading north into tulips
which way the wind blows
that way we venerate
fragrant bursts of orange and red
gently touching
oceans of systems—
there were pictures of smoke
and peaks emerging
from what used to be my eyes

Deceased Makers

In search of a clear spot in that winter wandered the votaries of seeds, sprouts, and dews, carrying suitcases, emptying pots, suggesting modifications. When "you" equals "us" by promise performed, they remember. Their bodies are stepping stones and clappers in bells. Now go and fetch some nice fruit. Not *you* actually, but a beautiful bird larger than a sparrow, with painted feet and collyrium.

Dyes/Explosives

Available thresholds were to extend no further than swifts, pigeons, and commercial storage—I went downstairs to see trees almost sideways, in a cloud that grew for a hundred miles. Walking back through quiet streets, I thought about the grass and its chemical content, then paused near the parking lot, so that those who move the highest generations could touch at the moment of transfer. A little river ran sweeping along.

The Actionlands

so it did not seem to be an impression theatres
parking then all three cross the street in clouds
and should they wake that night
I turn the threads for them
better not to concede they engage my attention
concerned by what would spring up in B
I paint them out
gradually toughening tissues
they might have entailed
had they split the remainder
                   driving north colorless
          repair shop of sloping fields
confirms this, plaid sorcerer—
that's his bike—losing vivacity
now hanging from one deadlocked nail
adjusted for wind and rain
then crushed face-to-face
for a pattern in stones
flipped up
are you
the light is pink

the moments glide between us
ready to be folded
the carved eye is open
the first and last tree
is marked in blue
toxicity

pour out air inexhaustible in its subdivisions
call across emerging strangers
then
    Are no more seen
touch it intimately and in its whole essence
the last known surface
piled on a truck under the pale awning
as my foot goes numb
and may afterwards become
the foundation of belief
to rest
in blossoms
not exactly narrowing
what unstrung you
punching through
the
    white-lipped
          sea

a blend of argument and assertion
is ferried in pails
to a tangle of trash
near the saplings
recalled from infancy
lights have
floated
through this zone
are you sure your bits of glass
glitter in the morning sun
limited to what I call
the art of it
being in it
and in that
holding a phrase
until it disappears

despite hope
to retain sensations
I see their heads only
lined up at the door
I have a duty to appear credible
my sight arrested by what's
in this pile of sand
loose love
even as refined glances
pass through our feet

all within target range
to be dropped off
at faerylond specifically
where out-of-state counsel
fills a giant urn
with the elder's
magnetic remains
leaving only the moist surfaces
of the colonnades
to differentiate
oh for
a smokeless paradise of which the memory is still fresh
nothing inside—no one talking
in some figurative way
antennae
quiver

what wouldn't Hecuba have done
what wouldn't she have done
had she known or understood

the most trivial facts of the seabed

having shaved her head and set forth
houseless to beg

would she have been cooled, quenched
like a seafarer of whom it may be possible
to say by what wind

                    craving and blazing

exactly

        would transition come

when everything

             wastes

for want of definition
fool

    there's a fool in my pocket
where the hen's teeth were
where the rainwater
sleeps now thirteen years
and you proceed upon one luminous quality

how to navigate the turmoil of that
with help from the objective ones
who delegate navigation to others

under cover of fog, the locked door
generates heat

             sublimely parked

beside the exit

                    that toy
                is the seal of god
        gliding on its back, rusting and flaking

and so less sensible of our
miserable condition
and you may have observed this
or paused to consider what is the nature
of that inference, then labored to uphold it
like stones on the hillside in spring
wrapped up in tape
rippling from our conception
or what it can motivate
collapsing, not extending
its defect into these

looking for something to define them
in respect of their unusual beauty
goosebumps on water-skin
gravel mixed with feed
to ennoble them
shadows passing in another room

I noticed a spider
raw and feather-tipped
eating
dried vegetables

on a circular bench
painted green—
I looked at the flower
and then no longer did
and those who watch, watch
and those who listen, listen
out of their blood our senses flow
and sound of Glinton bells
and piles of rusted hinges
leading out of the sun
but the bells were inaudible
so I turned off the light
when things had cleared
I saw the sky shining
underneath the grass

3

Middleless

looking east without pictures
diffusing themselves
that dreamless season
invested power
in half-closed eyes
moving on tiptoe
along the steepening curve
of the last book of stars
the torn skin
and colorless bones
waking to sense—
nerves concealed
between visualizations
rain rounding into sweat again

an obligation then arose
when a tenant stood
between the teachings
of the Old Academy
and the sun embroidered
with birdlike shapes

that all may gaze
on the white grass
of an ineluctable prime
converted for body
flashing across body
in ripe circles falling
use upon use
and centerless

five of us walking in memory
apart from orange plastic region
long ago clings to me
the freshly paynted gate
steps to an older rule
they'd almost wandered off
the dead spot, brushing my coat
in repose, as the tight circle
beats conjoined but not connected
alienated but to whom
upon a flower shine intricate
spice crowns, wraiths of
apples, squashed
pits, leaps of the sea

I die a little each day
but meet no obstruction
neither frequented nor seen

this may be the field
to which *mine* refers
you'd once walked here
on the high pavement—
either to touch you lightly
or go back to sleep
offers no increase in knowledge
not subsequently gained
by staying awake and listening
for the corners of the room
to take shape out of a dream

manyffold: this dares not money or property be engaged
nor now be propounded should one make out well
representing the power to you of an automatically acquired
carnal imagination—how far are we free through facilitating
expressions to determine when to be frozen given an
adequate selection of times, somewhat odd I makes the
opposite mistake save on behalf of those that had no right
before, but now are come to a permanent fixed interest in
something other than themselves, secluded here smelling
of tar one might be inclined to ask how is it your legs were
bent back by simplification one might reply the formula
requires a gesture like this, correlated with riches, honors,
pleasures, lawyers, armies, it does not extend beyond
them though perhaps it does, having become a spider

leaves and flowers lean
over a pit
a cold mouth grows wide
I forget which one
was pure cornfield above
leaching words
or were lost or had felt so
on the broad waters
where one assumes it might
be useful if they would stop
I knew from what had been posited
whether by mistake or by necessity
that nobody else knew
where is kind treatment now?

the potential acquisition of body eases
concerns in this calm the lasting
prodigality of the unchosen
intertwines with matter
as residue of the fixed sphere
vests in an infant
at the same anomalous point
although rational, what I
could not say when confronted
with observed facts—there was once
a time—or subsidence of the future—
when the rational was pain

and everything nested inside it
no easy thing, but I could adjust to that

this part is divided in four parts
which are mechanically coated
then sent off to convince
by virtue of their arrangement
in lieu of further argument—
stretched along the bridge
from subject to predicate
given a voice accepted
for genuine should
descendants survive
the effects of smoke in-
fused with hard work
after hearing talk burn
clear and determinate trees

air lifting out smoke the gear in cliffs
now dips for sun and the making of
the file, does it approach three lit
flowers weaving seriatim wheels
covinous and tossing themselves up
they feigneth so vast a distance
so clear an expanse, reasonably
here also, the tail slants
across the blue square's distinct

ranges—after cutting out
the stain, the floor is revealed
trailing pathetically along
my parents clog the farebox
I am everywhere they look

those lines on Monday will be awful
whatever system we embrace
if the mind arose by vegetation
working through unenjoyed
possession of eyes
to scatter them inside
a body, whose missing
shape is annexed
each spring, blood racing
through all creatures
like a shining chain—ready to be
annihilated, the activities
they produce adapt to the phrases
in which I express them

medieval cinnamon trust of the sign
subaqueous vaults suspended—
my head is aware but forgets to
maintain control over its ideas
Magnum, Medium, Parvum, Minimum
yielding total xylenes to endure

by reason of vagrant shadows
dug side by side
the tracks form circles in descent
where you remove your boots
I turn to multiplication, mercy, humility,
patience, pity, and each of their correlatives
intending the following rules be used
to order them, then wash them away

the heavy, the sad, the smooth, the rough, the bitter,
the hard, the wicked, the brief, the coarse, the loud,
the hidden, the warm, the recumbent, the astringent
whether transmutation of sweat into air
signifies the middle of unrealized thought
by lease and release of interest
in what we call things
not anxious to be combined
by cold estimation none
to sweep up after the crazed, the shaken
those prepared to sacrifice
through imaginative or sensitive power
the flavor, the sweetness none
could describe except the enflamed

temporary weird report waits for me
I figure our response had not been extant
or might have been attuned

to the true sense of an instrumental
cause outside privation of past and future—
so why adopt this attitude
when there's no doubt, opening drawers
bristling with dust and stammering
strangely in defiance
of the supreme principle
but composed of rival substance
having expelled all attachment
living in salt of sun and null light
a garden they thought was a fire

memory terminates in facts summoned by
weakness of present impressions—it may
be proper to remark perpendicularly that in
practicing divination the tongue can waste away
with its own moisture streaming out before it
fully exposed to everything
even when chopped in pieces
custom asserts wings
swollen in thickets where tall clouds
cleverly turn into fish
swimming with downcast eyes in
the dark, concise and elegant
the smoky fluid becomes a voice
forming the fatal speech of fish

customary pressure applied
to cloth that may have fallen
as reflected sunlight fades
into wires overhead
deep blue, clotted
blue, ultramarine
having crept through
grain again
we retreat in pairs
the tenth and last step
contrary to sensation
having potential to betray
sleepless trust imposing
each on us in semidarkness

jellies moon and sea and dry flocks of fish jaws
with legs and feet and dark green veins split
into blunt fields with faces
touched by many textures blending
thousands of years on the outcrop
meeting eyes transformed
from rows of teeth
ascending the cloudlike stair
and mountains of old speech
above Palenque near the sea the fish
pleased by the words in which
their pleasures were spoken

through the fourfold eyes of air
the land is almost visible

transferring past to future exactly as
footprint follows the common freedom
of the earth in gray forests permanently
pale common colors return from India
in what shape information takes looking
down by light of natural philosophy
at the base of the head which could
freely turn along the bare edge
of fried neckbones in deep
consideration contriving listeners
to appear from the earth
walking rapidly
then cut in two at every word
so shed tongue tears

middleless the furrowed bitter
beware the power of the bitter
recited continuously above
that enters the heart the
acrid air that stirs
others odorless at evening
and those that do not yield
rise up translucent

for bread to be shared
and glazed with refinements
amethyst clicks lightly
on the automatic door
and rings nor middle
nor end nor begins